Trapezing in the Dark
Poetic flights through inner space

Mary Lister

Front cover: Painting by Diana Henderson © 2018
Edited by: Polly Walker
ISBN: 9798371006226
Copyright @ 2022, Mary Lister

Dedication
To my husband Ken,
my Far East and my Wild West,
and my fellow traveller through life and books.

Contents

Trapezing in the Dark   1
For the love of travel and landscape   3
Stone Sofas of West Nab   5
The Stone Giant Rises   6
The Great Famine Memorial: Clew Bay, County Mayo   7
Statues - a Test of our Times   8
Up on the Buddha's Head: Bamiyan in Afghanistan   9
West Lake at Hangzhou (Naming Nature)   11
Yangshuo in the Rain   12
Yellow Mountains   13
Tsingy Tsong   14
Chitral Valley, Pakistan: The Polo Match   15
Ta Prohm, Angkor Wat   16
Inca!   17
Shadows on the Niger   18
Dogon Country, Mali   20
Walking the Dog in Vermont, Through Four Seasons   21
Titicaca: Where Men Knit   23
Chiloé: Where Women Knit   24
Deep Purple Lake in Bolivia   25
Women of Afghanistan   26
False Justice. Mahsa Amini, Iranian Martyr   27
Lapland   28
Midnight Sun   29
Swan of Tuonela   31
Lake Avernus and the Sybil's Cave at Cumae   33
Midwinter St Lucia   34
Sculpture Park   36
The Northern Lights, Beyond Words   37
Walls   38
Ping Pong with Zoroastrians   39
Cello Song   40
Postcard From the Future   41
Landscapes in Colour   42
For the love of myths and history   43
Ragnarök (the Icelandic End of the World)   45
Questions   46
The Library of Babel – Decoding the Secrets of the Universe 48
Alternative Histories: Making History a Bit Nicer   50
After Homer: A New Odysseus - Mandela.   52

Totem Song of the Northwest 53
Branwen the Raven 55
Medusa, Set in Stone 56
The Lion Statuette, 40,000 years BC 57
King Arthur Wakes 58
The Horses of Byzantium 61
Shakespeare's Villains, on the Touchy Subject of Remorse 62
At the Existentialist Café with Apricot Cocktails 64
Human Racehorses 66
Mount Olympus 67
Death, the Stalker (after Emily Dickinson) 69
La Mer 70
The Pythia: Priestess of Delphi 71
Silkie Ascending 72
History in Blues 73
Sun – the Shining One, Comes to Tea 74
Prufrock in Lockdown 2020 76
The Emperor Whisperer 78
For the love of Love **81**
Geography Lovers 83
Ethical People Smuggler 84
Two Armchairs on a Hebridean Beach 86
Early Spring 87
Archaeology of Self 88
The Old Bed 89
Inner Landscapes 91
Sekhmet, a Talisman 93
Franklin's Song 94
Diana's Garden 96
The Mother 97
Moon Breath 98
Snow 99
Goldfinch Child 100
The Window 101
The Box of Delights 102
It's Gone: The Inner Landscape of Dementia 103
Songs from Story of the Earth **105**
The Insects' Song 107
The Bird Song 108
Bio-Diversity Hoe Down 109
The Reptile Song 110

Trapezing in the Dark

I lurch precarious between the poles,
balance on trembling feet before I leap.
Below me, only vertigo of life,
above me whirls a vortex of pulsating stars.
I circle weightless in the space between
light and dark, dark and light,
suspended upside-down, no compass point.
Feeling the wind in every air-born arc,
curving towards the infinite and back,
I am trapezing in the dark.

Mortality sits heavy on us all.
Gravity is the only sane response.
Why, oh why, do I feel this strange surge of joy,
this pulse of light, this primal spark,
as I swing forward on such fragile threads?
I am trapezing in the dark.

One tiny thread connects me
to all things as I float, and glide,
an acrobat of existential space.
I only trust that I can catch and grasp the flying rope,
the trailing hand.
Who knows but that the next leap will be my last,
the last curve of the moving part
trapezing into light.

For the love of travel and landscape

Stone Sofas of West Nab

Dark crags and boulders are atlases
starkly shouldering the lowering sky.
You can hear their groans on the wind,
mingled with the ghost cry of the lapwing.

The stone sofas on Meltham Moor
gather rain in their abandoned seats.
Once granite giants sat watch over the dark landscape,
till dawn sent them striding back
beneath the earth to their peat caverns
in carboniferous Valhallas, under the high swell of the moors.

Perhaps once Moai and Colossi came from distant lands,
swilled dark beer from millstone cups,
and sang the world into being with their Pennine cousins.
But things turned uncordial at midnight, and in a drunken spat,
rocks got hurled and scattered.
Then the stone cock crowed on the Cock Crowing Stone
in that dawn of time.
All turned to millstone grit, all petrified.

The landscape is the story
and the meaning.
I merely wander across
- Already a lost strand of narrative
In its mythic geology.

The Stone Giant Rises

The moors are our giant bed, soft and yielding
for my giantess and me.
We sleep down centuries.
One night is a hundred years on our peat moss mattress.
Rocks are our stony pillows, in textured layers,
and the Earth moves as we mumble and turn in slumber.

There she lies, sleep-eyes crusted and lichened,
moaning soft as the moorland wind
as she dreams of storms flitting like flies
through our open skylight.
Now I will rise and hunt,
tripping and snapping wire traps on poles,
trampling stone dwellings, and bright metal beetles
underfoot, with silver bees droning round my head.
I will find a river for my giantess to quaff,
I'll forage the landscape for green forest porridge,
and purple-heathered honeydew,
and fresh boulders for my giantess to crunch
with her monolith teeth for her once-a-century breakfast.

Then, risen and revived, we will stride,
hand in stone hand,
across England's less pleasant, less green, land.

The Great Famine Memorial: Clew Bay, County Mayo

Now a ragged ship of death stands
where they once embarked for a new life.
Skeletal sails on skeleton mast,
half-flagged and weighed down with bronze cargo.
But those left behind died too.
Wind, rain, and potato rot took them
on a longer journey, in their slow bite
down the dark gorge of the grave.

The old woman watched the ship sail from Clew Bay
between the Mayo mountains,
her son, and all her hopes, on board.
She stood till night took the horizon,
till she was alone with the prolonged sigh of sea on shore,
and the churn of hunger waves
wearing her from within,
heaving and tearing at her gut.

New journeys have been made to these parts,
child soldiers from the Congo,
sent by some distant diplomatic handshake,
to learn or re-learn humanity.
They live out rain-soaked job-seekers lives
in a landscape pock-marked by roofless ruins,
abandoned by those who left,
bereft of all humanity, long ago.
Homesickness hangs like rags of sail
in the grey air.

Statues - a Test of our Times

Oh Jan Reid, heroine indeed!
Gloriously quick to leap
in full dark resin
on to the slaver's plinth!
We cannot have heroes
made of the cloth of slavery
forged like chains in faraway fields,
or the part-slavery of the mill.

But we must never forget,
as we sit-pretty in our arts,
that slavery is alive today
as ever – even more than ever.
That fist raised in triumph
is silent, though it bursts through forms –
To this the poet must add a voice
and music, a soundtrack.
I am not for tearing down reminders.
Not for hiding memories.

But I am for writing, fresh and new,
a more loving, compassionate future.

Up on the Buddha's Head: Bamiyan in Afghanistan

Mile after mile
in ancient, grinding, coloured buses
crammed with people, fruit, and goats.

We travelled surreal landscapes
of moon mountains and sun deserts,
to come to Bamiyan Valley.

There, distantly seen,
like teeth in the mouths of cliffs
stood two gargantuan red Buddhas
framed by a mountain range
of infinite blue and mauve, and soft pinks.

Carved by Buddhist hands,
marking a gentler empire that stretched
from India to Afghanistan, to China,
to the worlds of desert chieftains, nomads, kings.
Through the arteries of merchant and marauder.
- trade and raid along the Silk Road.

Arab invaders stormed Bamiyan in their path,
in the seventh century, long ago.
They obliterated the gentle gazing faces
of the giants - tore out the eyes
that gazed across the valley floor.
shattered the mouths that spoke in eloquent silence.

We reached the giant feet, alone.
and mounted up the steep dark corridors
and stairways carved in the cliffs by monks long gone,
to stand at last, upon the Great Buddha's head.
We gazed from those sightless eyes above that blanked out
face -
through a camera lens.

Then far below we heard a distant shout,
as an ant to Goliath, a tiny waving speck below.
"No photo! Forbidden! No photo! No!"
We have the shot to prove it.
Was it too sacred? Too potent to be trod by pilgrims, even
then?

Time passed. The Taliban blew the Buddhas up
with stark remorseless blasts.
Not just their eyes and mouths now-
They burned tyres on that head we stood on,
explosives in each limb. A sad start to a new hopeful
Millennium.
All of them blown to dust, across the valley floor.
I feel them as dust in my own eye now, blown in the wind.
Look on my Works ye Mighty... they are gone

West Lake at Hangzhou (Naming Nature)

Where Moon reflects on Three Pools
and scarlet goldfish swirl like autumn flames,
I sat by the Pagoda of Winter Snow on Shining Bridge,
to contemplate the poetry of Chinese names.

The emperors of the Southern Song in ancient times
sat pensively in dragon boat on Mirrored Lake.
Musicians delicately plucked their flutes of harmony and light
where glowing sky meets earth, and silver waters break.

And painters of swift brush strokes and steady hand
magic-ed up the Mountains Flying from Afar,
moons that smiled on lovers destined soon to part,
and rippling bamboo forests of the falling star.

The gods with bulging eyes and cosmic winds
blew kindly breezes through the Blossomed Gardens of
Delight,
while empresses and dancing long-sleeved girls
sang poetry in pagodas long into celestial night.

This vision rose before my eyes on Mirrored Lake,
the misty silhouette of temple roof on distant hill.
I saw those emperors pass, like history, in their painted dragon
boats,
and knew that China has its poetry still.

Yangshuo in the Rain

Black, white, and shades of grey
are the colours chosen by the ancient Chinese
painters of scrolls.
The minimal lines of the magically shaped karst mountains
are misted in washes of grey
with the slightest of brush-strokes -
suggesting, not showing, the mystical landscapes
of the heavenly kingdom
inhabited by the gods.
And that is exactly what we see
as we bike through the drizzling rain
of the cold Yangshuo morning -
Just the merest hints drawn in the mist,
of ghostly peaks in wispy apparitions,
looming behind the grey-day tones,
with reflected light on the rain-drenched paddy fields,
where the water-buffalo with glassy eyes
watch us pass.

Chinese women in coolie hats
halt our mud-splattered bikes
to sell us postcards of what
we might see on a blue-green summer day.
But we pedal on through reflective puddles,
preferring our shades of mist and grey.

Yellow Mountains

Like real birds on silver mechanical wires
we soar up to the peaks of the Yellow Mountains,
that hold up heaven.
Those 'mountains that fly from afar…'

There, ancient pines sculpted by winds
and whirling mists,
into shapes of the dancing spirits of the Tang Dynasty,
guide us to the summit.

And there we meet the Chinese gods
for tea rituals with picnic cups.
Under a full moon we gaze down on Mirror Lake,
Jade temple, and Forbidden Cities.

At dawn we descend on a cloud
and play Mahjong in a café,
with smiling men in white vests
who laugh at our dream journey.

Tsingy Tsong

I saw it in the National Geographic.
The Tsingy of Madagascar,
An ancient seabed of karst pinnacles,
like a hundred miles of cathedrals sticking out of a jungle far
away,
a limestone labyrinth.
I must reach the summit where the sifakas and lemurs leap,
and rare fish eagles surveille the valley -
overcoming all my vertigo.
I had to go. I knew I must go.
We set off in a pirogue, a hollow log, down the River
Tsiribihina.
From there an oxcart ride to the foot.

200-foot-high forest of metallic spires
that sound at the touch, like organ pipes.
Touch the jagged spikes and they sing, and echo with a song.
Edging up jagged edges, sharp as razors
roped on cables and clicking crampons,
step by painful step,
my vertigo in check, so high my desire,
till we reached the summit belvedere
and gazed like the eagles across the vast expanse
of jutting jagged summits stretching into the far distance
of the Madagascan Forest.
There the lemurs leapt, and golden sifakas danced
from spiney peak to razor point
where prehistoric fish once swam.
And there at last the Tsingy Tsung to me.

Chitral Valley, Pakistan: The Polo Match

We were following in Alexander's footsteps,
Trish Mir in the distance, like a mirage of promise,
a shining snow-tipped beacon.

We descended steeply down into the wide green valley -
Welcome after a week of bouncing in an ancient jeep
over the hostile grey verticals of the Hindu Kush.

Along the precipitous tracks, often fallen away,
over Lowari Top, with the driver's 24 cousins hanging on
in a pyramid of acrobats, like a bizarre circus act.

All smiling, in Chitrali hats, rifles strung at their backs-
You don't argue with cousins like that
in the remotest place on earth. You smile back.

Suddenly we heard a riot of sound below us in the valley.
Two clashing orchestras, competing for cacophony.
two audiences' frenzied cheers,
two polo teams of thundering ponies.

Tribal riders, Chitral versus Kafiristan, turbans streaming,
swinging mallets, swooping, whacking, whooping, steaming
after a goat's bladder tied with string.

Trumpets snarled staccato blares, from one end,
then the other.
Drums rattled, cymbals clashed, bagpipes droned.
2 Orchestras antiphonal, in conflict, chaos and triumph.
A war of music. A rush of joy. A welcome in a faraway place.

Ta Prohm, Angkor Wat

Stone apsaras dance in ancient shrines.
Only the strangler fig trees octopian roots
dance with them through time in their slow petrified joy,
to the rhythms of centuries,
played out now by an orchestra of landmine victims
of the new Khmer reign.

Framed in giant strangling tendrils,
doorways open to other worlds, dark and cool,
leading through endless corridors,
archwayed in surreal punctuation,
to a Buddha,
where three orange-robed monks bring flowers
from this world to the next.
I touch a gargantuan fig–root.
Guardian or epiphyte?

The Khmer Rouge fled here, fading into jungle myth
after their raids on the killing fields.
Were they unmoved by this numinous place,
by the sensuous joy of the stone dancers?
Did these roots never hold them to account
in their slow-moving strangling caress?
Did the Buddha sit in his private contemplation
and never touch their dark enjungled hearts?

Inca!

The Spanish never found it -
too weighed down with armour and stolen Inca gold.
The Incas kept silent about their hidden city in the clouds.
Now tourist buses plough up the sides
in steep vertiginous kirby-grip bends endlessly up a vertical.
And suddenly we are there in the Andean sky,
looking down on clouds,
from a perfect templed city, each inch terraced,
and cultivated, beneath the condor's watchful eye.
We caught the last bus down,
noticing a steep stone staircase straight down the cliff,
between the winding bends, 52 hairpins
fit only for the fleet-footed, and the brave-hearted.
"Inca!" A shout like a challenge, a paean of triumph,
a small boy in red, red-feathered plume on his headband,
saluted us as we drove past between bends
from the lower step of the rock face.
He was there again at the next staircase.
"Inca" he yelped, as we trundled downwards.
And then at the next. - Such fearless agility,
like an incarnation of Quetzalcoatl.
"Inca!" He ran -or flew- down each level,
saluting at each base-step, arms like a wide-spread flag.
Twenty or more times – "INCA!" ... "INCA!"
The Incas lived again. He was the hero of their ancient empire.
We cheered him every time. We cheered the Inca People,
not lost or destroyed, not dead,
but alive and flying down the cliff face of the lost city.
An embodiment of indestructible history.
Only later we discovered that he was not one boy, but twenty.
Each ran down just one staircase of stone steps, like a relay.
Twenty Inca boys, with fierce eagle faces,
and the red plumes on their heads –
But they shared their reward from us.
Then took their bow as one people. INCAS!

Shadows on the Niger

The moon draws dapples on the glassy waters of the Niger.
A kora plays on the midstream stage.
The Festival of the Niger.
Nearby, in a sheltered courtyard I have set a triptych of screens:
a shadow theatre in the dark.
The torches are lit, illuminating the audience like silhouettes, in rows.
We lift our apparitions, incubus monsters of nightmare,
with cut out features, jewelled like stain-glass, purple, red and blue.
The story begins, in French.
I have dedicated my tale to Toumani Diabate,
a Griot praise singer of 200 generations, he tells me.

Now hellish hyena-men with snapping jaws,
leopard devils, and hippo-horrors, arch across the screens.
Seven masked men emerge dancing, from stygian corners.
We snarl, we howl, caterwaul and whoop
in the international language of nightmare,
the linguistics of Tartarus, the chorale of the Apocalypse.
But this is Africa. This is Mali.
It's a story about a goddess, Kora, who first creates music,
and the whole music tradition of the Mandinka Nation.

We hear a plink of a string, the resonance of a gourd.
It was the first magical kora, or so I spin my tale,
that subdued the monsters that lurked in darkness.
She enchanted them with the primal music of the world.
They howl melodically, despite their wickedness,
despite their fevered wildness,
and find themselves dancing to the rhythms of beauty,
and the harmony of nature.
They grin with their hideous visages, and sing love songs, not hate.

The masked men and the shadow puppets change
in slow motion, the audience entranced, move slowly,
spellbound across the courtyard floor.

The Storyteller names the Kora the Divine Instrument of Mali,
and that this music would transmogrify all evil.
The audience rise and clap
Then I gather up my shadow monsters
to dance again one day.
But the soulful song of Kora lingers resonant
across the shadow of the Niger.

Dogon Country, Mali

You climb down the high Bandiagara Escarpment
to reach the Dogons,
in sandstone villages of peaked pepper-pot houses
backed against caves and tombs carved in cliff walls.
They fled here long ago, escaping conversion, or slave traders,
to remain Animists, the Nommo, sons of Amma, their god.

You can hear the rustle of restless ancestors,
and the eerie echoes of birds calling,
as you sleep on the roofs, under the stars.
Their architecture, art and ritual hold their secret history.
Carved granary doors encapsulate their culture and beliefs.
Village elders gather under low-thatched meeting halls.
Startling stilt- walkers in masks summon their forebears
to protect the spirits of the departed. Their ancestral presence
is palpable.

This is the Sigi, a ritual rarely performed,
and we are here.
The masked dancers in flamboyant purple and red grasses,
on high stilts, are wonderfully, surreally strange –
Bird-like, bull-like, animalistic, atavistic…ani-mystical.
They dance out a whole cosmology in movement.
Scientists and anthropologists hotly debate
the Dogon mythic knowledge of Sirius B, and all the stars.
But the mysterious ceremony dances, chants
enchants you to other places.
This is the other world, and we are its witnesses.
Can I summon up those moments under their stars in mere words?

Walking the Dog in Vermont, Through Four Seasons

Luminous vermillion maples
glowed startling in the mist,
rustling torchbearers holding flames
to guide us on early morning walks.

Except I ran mostly, dragged on a leash
by our She-Hound Sheba, She-Dog, huge as Anubis,
Hell-bent, wild, in free fall,
drawing Isis, I, from my profiled high feathered pace.

Scorching liquid crimson,
falling through Fall
surreal and intense,
hung from dawn in pure form -
the essence of *red*.

I, with my Isis eye, leaf-peeping,
drawn through fire and mist towards the light,
by Anubis, the Black Dog's daughter,
all questing-nosed excitement, unstoppable.

Soon, those dancing flames
turned to ice-silhouettes against the swirling snow.
White, white now, as Winter fell, sudden as a trip switch.
Now I skied, leash in gloved hands
behind the She-Hound, Moose-Harrier, Deer-Huntress of darkness,
questing black-nosed through snow blindness.

The hushed swish swish of the skis breaking the silence
round the track between white mountains,
till we crossed the resonance of the covered bridge,
like a drawn-out drum-roll,
to the Christmas lights of the little white town.

And just as suddenly white Winter melted into mud
under the blue sky, and we were running
in a verdigris world of green mountains
purple and magenta-fringed.
A humid mauve haze rose from the earth in a new spectrum,
igniting a touch-paper palette of colour for Spring and
Summer.

I with my Isis eye, up from the underworld, fully in ascension,
led by Anubis' daughter questing and wet-nosed,
snuffling the secret tracks of racoons,
or swerving to the beaver dams along the stream
now banked with yellow flecks like candles.

I, now, new-eyed, new-nosed, new-eared,
dog-led at full pace through the cycle of turning seasons.

Titicaca: Where Men Knit

There's an island where men knit
on Titicaca
Clickety-click.

> They knit to woo
> They do,
> They knit to woo.
> Tickety-tick, on Titicaca,
> Clickety-click.

And lovely girls walk to and fro
looking at knitting as they go.
Men click their needles,
Clickety-click.
They stroll, or sit on walls to knit
patterned hats to warm their brides,
exquisite gloves and scarves besides.
Like weaver birds they ply their skill.
Girls know at once to say, "I will",
from tiny patterns they decide
to choose a mate and be their bride.
For knitting is the role of Man.
A transcendental gift - or plan,
more than a mating ritual this:
A patterned pathway to a kiss.

> They knit to woo.
> They really do.
> And then they knit for babies too,
> on Titicaca's shores, it's true.
> Survival skills writ in alpaca,
> llama wool and fur of guanaca.
> Clickety-click, clickety-click,
> Tickety-tick, tickety-tick,
> on Titicaca where men knit.

Chiloé: Where Women Knit

Chilotes live on stilt-legged houses
that walk the sea
wrapped in grey mists of the Pacific shore.

And there, women knit with great skeins of wool
the colours of earth and ocean,
flecked and syncopated with the indigo
and crimsons of houses.
Patterns and codes speak the rhythms of the sea,
inherited through a thread of ancestors and grandmothers
down the mitochondrial line, woven in their very DNA.

> I walked the desolate beach
> warm in ochre and grey, the colours
> of lichen on stone, pebble on sand,
> seaweed on rock.

Darwin walked here once
thinking of evolution and survival.
Did he spot the passing of genes in the patterned wool?
Or survival of the fittest in the intricate code of pearl and plain,
the artistry of the women's designs
in the grand design of things?

> Did he stop like me,
> to buy a sweater from a woman by the road –
> ochre and grey, flower and stone?
> Her great great grandmother perhaps, sold him the same,
> to warm him on the Beagle's lonely journey
> along the frozen shores and glaciers of Patagonia?

Deep Purple Lake in Bolivia

It was deep purple. I wasn't dreaming.
A purple lake as far as the eye could see,
with graduations of colour
from dark aubergine, magenta, crimson, red.

High altitude! My nostrils breathed in ice and salt
off the altiplano,
as I walked the purple fringes,
and my head sung.

A thousand delicate sunrise pink flamingos
stood, dipping their bills
into the volcanic waters,
sifting the chemic slime.
The lake echoed with their conversations,
and the flutter of wings as they flapped or settled.

Later that night, we walked under the Milky Way,
so low in the sky we could reach up
to pluck diamonds like orchard fruits overhead.

We came to a shop, a shack on the lonely shore,
run by a Maputo woman in a bowler hat.
On the sparse shelves just biscuits and lemonade,
and a stack of armadillos. Nothing more.

We wandered back along the dark purple waters,
to our tin hut, where we huddled,
zero at the bone,
in sleeping bags joined up,
through a Bolivian night.
This time I was dreaming. In deep purple.
But real life is more surreal.

Women of Afghanistan

Oh, lovely women of Afghanistan,
I light a candle for you tonight.
I keep vigil for you
under the starry sky that stretches beyond me to you,
bonding us, sisters.
Your lovely faces…
Will they be de-faced, like the Buddhas of Bamiyan?
Be dehumanised, smudged into faceless nobodies,
into… Nothing?
You are more than them,
these hair-shirted joyless scarecrows
that dare question their own god's loveliest creation?
Woman. Women. Lovely women. Womankind.
Lovers, mothers, daughters, voices of peace.

Your lovely voices, singing the ancient music of Afghanistan,
may be silenced.
Your hands set to slavery.
Denied education.
Your lovely eyes, watchful through your textured prison bars,
may see horrors unimaginable.
And your lovely feet
may never run you free, out of your land,
across the sea.
Oh, lovely women of Afghanistan,
my tears are flowing out to you tonight.
The candle flickers. It must not go out…

False Justice. Mahsa Amini, Iranian Martyr

September 2022

What court saw your trial? Your death penalty?
None but the 'Morality' Police.
They roughed you up
when they saw your lovely face
and lustrous hair...
Called you 'whore'
that their god had made you so beautiful.
And when they finished,
and all had had their turn,
they beat you up some more
and left you dead.
Judgement by state-sponsored violence
against girls, lovers, mothers.
The Morality Police were judge, jury, executioner,
and their verdict was you had... a medical condition...
Beauty.
Veils are torn and burned.
Blood flows and flows...

Lapland

In the wilderness,
we threaded the woodland floor on a narrow path.
Lichen and moss, mushrooms and toadstools mile after mile -
a hundred forms of fungus sprung from logs, and fallen trees
- till we were mesmerised.

Suddenly, without warning, the forest floor
fell into a new dimension, like a hologram.
It turned into a tapestry, woven and spun in high definition.
The moss, a thousand shades of green, and yellow and gold,
was punctuated by scarlet lichens. Van Gogh splashes of
vivid vermillion, ochre, red, oranges and pinks -
a great unfolding carpet of colour, texture and shape
seemed to spread infinitely into the horizon from beneath our
feet.

Sensitive to our tread
as a woven bridge,
undulating at each footfall.
We were tightrope-walking
on Einstein's flexible curving structures.
through multi-dimensional space.

I saw each detail, every frond of fern,
each delicate dappled leaf,
each parded mushroom and mossy crevice
was painted, and pointillist.
I sensed each vibrant shade,
and smelled each dank dark earthy smell
of that wilderness,
as if on opiates.

Midnight Sun

We sailed into the Midnight Sun
in a beautiful orange 'Longship' boat,
to Slartibartfast's frilly coasts.
The Vikings were our genial hosts…
served fishy delicacies on toasts.
We ate till we could barely float.

Across the dark blue Arctic seas
we journeyed to Lofoten's Isles
where towering mountains fringe fjords.
And even there the Viking hoards
welcomed us with Nordic cheese,
and conquered us with winning smiles.

Then Tromso, darkest Arctic town,
held a Festival of Light,
where teams dressed up in crazy garb-er
to race in boats across the harbour,
oars churning water up and down.
Huge crowds turned out to watch the sight.

Ladies with jellyfish heads and masks
rowed longboats versus Ancient Greeks.
Ibsen's Women versus Greig's grim Trolls,
each dressed according to their roles,
and each performed their heaving tasks
'gainst Vikings, robots, boffins, geeks.

So, in my dreams I will return
to midnight revels in the Sun.
Our average age was 'half-deceased'.
We loved Valhalla's sunlit feasts.
'Viking' is just a word to note,
people plunderin' in a boat…
so now a Viking I've become.

And when Valhalla gently calls
from mountains and from waterfalls,
I know now what awaits us there:
Sunlit feasts and such delights
as dancing in the Northern Lights,
and shining in the atmosphere.

Swan of Tuonela

I longed to return to Suomi,
to the Finnish forests and lakes.
So, I called aloud to the wild trees,
the Rowan, the Birch, and the Oak.
"Who will give me wood to make
a fine sledge, with a slicing edge,
a sleigh to carry me on my way
that can double as flight, or float?
- A transport light as a swan's feather
bound with elk and reindeer leather?"

The copper Rowan whispered,
murmured in the wind and sighed.
"Not I, not with my wood or copper berries,
I must watch over water and air.
The gold Oak shuddered its golden leaves,
"Nor I … I am too stern, too rooted firm,
with stout arms that reach the sky."

But the silver Birch shivered, sighed and quivered,
"Take my wood, I'm one of many, many am I.
My roots are of Karelian chants,
my rustling leaves Sibelian dance,
the Kantele my branches high."
I made of her a fine long sleigh,
a flying sledge, light as a feather
that soared like music in the wind.

And I was on my way
to the lands of Sariola, of Pohjola, the Northern lands
where the sun can barely shine
one hour in every day.
I met with Vainamoinen then, inscrutable, a man of myth,
Spirit of Water, and frozen lakes,

with the Sampo in his hands.
"You only have a little time,
a moment here, a passing dream.
Your journey takes you on
to the darker lands of Tuonela,
the Shadowlands, the Isle of Death.
Your time is nearly done."

Then Vainamoinen helped me search
for a snowshoe made of birch, a leather belt of reindeer hide,
the black feather of the sacred swan....
A perturbation on the lake,
a rippling shadow in blackness bleak.
The Swan of Tuonela flew down,
with an oboe sound, a haunting horn,
and a swansong in its beak.
I clung around its downy neck,
cradled in its feathered wings.

We took flight among the scudding clouds,
billowing, torn as tattered shrouds.
Forests and frozen lakes below
seemed scattered as we flew.
We came at last to Tuonela,
Hel's home, isle of bones,
of grey wraiths, and flitting ghosts
and jutting standing stones.

I have no Lemmenkainen tricks,
and no shape-shifting shaman power.
The light is taken from my eyes
approaching this, my final hour.
I write this tale, these thoughts, this note,
traced on snow, soon melted, gone.
A message with no journey on -
with the black feather of that swan…
The Swan of Tuonela.

Lake Avernus and the Sybil's Cave at Cumae

It is A-Ornos - where the Birds don't sing -
a silent bubbling lake with sulphurous haze.
Even the Winds hold their breath.
Here in a cave, a poet saw the Sybil hanging upside down in a jar,
sending echoes to a Wasteland not yet born.
Here too, Aeneas, led by Vergil, heard the Sibyl's voice
through nine orifices in the rock,
sending him on a journey to find a golden bough
as passport to the underworld and back.
Rome's future rose or fell on her layered grace notes.
Long ago now, I came to this place
and sang like a tabooed bird,
Solveig's sad lament to her journeying Peer Gynt.
Thinking I was alone, I gave full throat to her song,
testing the truth of Vergil's words
about the nine voices echoing through apertures,
like nine harmonies of whispered prophecy.
Some German travellers were startled at the entrance
transported by the sound, hair on end, transfixed and rooted.
They heard my Sibyl song, weaving and spiralling along dark tunnels
like echoing fumes arising from Hades.
Who knows what prophecies they heard amplified
against the songless silent sky?
Later that night, sleeping in Apollo's temple nearby,
a local band rocked our silence in Avernus' starry night,
with a stilted wailing version of a Beatles' song:
'Letter B Let it Be, Letter B Let it Be –
There must be an Aunts-Wer, Letter B',
like a distorted bizarre parody of the Oracle's code.
Our own fates were already twisting in the Sibyl's Jar,
spelling out, letter by letter, by Linear B and letter B, our journeys
on into the future...

Midwinter St Lucia

So here we are,
washed up on Prospero's enchanted island,
wandering St Lucia in the midwinter heat,
with Walcott's Omeros,
(painter of words, poet sorcerer,) netted in a bag.
Curacao blue oceans
churn and churn at the white beach.
Too hot for anything but gazing lazy,
we sit sipping,
supping curacao blue-sea cocktails,
cupped from the sea.

I read of the gods thundering pianos,
and the hurling of furniture in the sky.
Then, we hear it. Tempest clouds, shipwreck breakers,
Cosmic trip-switching, lightning special effects,
kettledrums on tin rooves.
In the morning the beach has disappeared,
and we are marooned in vanished sorcery.

The Drive-in Volcano was not discussed by Shakespeare.
It is the gentle sulphurous womb of some goddess,
whose steeply rising breasts are the two Pitons.
Her head and whirling eddies of hair are undersea…
Those are pearls that were her eyes…

The fish learn new shades of brilliant in the pumice clear
water.
Snorkelled, we pass over their kingdoms
mapped by corals,
full-fathomed citadels of sea life,
hallucinogenic in dappled stripes and colours
beyond artists palettes.

Inland the lava-fertile soil enriches

forests and vegetation with essence of green-flowing
sweetness,
alive with birdsong and insect orchestras.
They sing of full-flowering fruit, extremes of yellow or red,
of seeds and seasons, and lush succulents
in the hazy spectrum of magical.

Frigate birds puff out red-balloon chests
in ecstasy of mating ritual.
All nature here dances and makes music.
Everything is in love.
We pass a wooden shack school with corrugated roof.
Two Nobel prize-winners went here,
one a poet, the other a mathematician -
boys incubating for a monochrome world beyond.

Surely only poets grow here, luminous word magicians,
rhapsodic painters of myth,
sitting on the seas' edge, poised on the curling wave,
inside the crucible of a storm?
What else is there to speak in, except poetry?

Sculpture Park

Sculptors hone wild rocks
into Nature's shapes, or galvanise steel in faraway forges
to make huge human forms -
Mankind made monumental in a landscape
beyond the human, beyond mortal.
Meanwhile the trees,
Nature's own artists and sculptors,
spring from the Earth in the wildest forms,
evolving from only seeds,
blown in the wind.

Elemental artists, self-inventing,
with painterly artlessness
write their own epics of land and sky,
sculpt with tortuous turns of branch and twig,
of root and bough,
Turner-prize defying exhibitions of Nature
beyond Capability with his naturalised tranquillity.
This is wild nature's art.

Tamed now, weighed down by children
swinging on their boughs, as if the trees
were just background exhibits to the main show:
the sculptures,
where thoughtful notices read,
"Do not climb on these man-made imitations
hewn from rock,
forged in bronze and steel".

The Northern Lights, Beyond Words

Whiteness, breathing through darkness.
Whiteness, exhaled in pointillist flakes.
We skied home across the fields
to the soft swish of snow.
Beyond, only the white noise of silence.
The massive spirits of trees
our looming companions, fully furred in ermine.
Ice kings silhouetted against black night.

Then the Aurora leapt into the sky,
dancing an undulating apocalypse.
We were in the palms of its enormity,
cradled in its lustrous arms, helpless, entranced.
The sky rustled its immense curtains
showing us its mysteries,
the theatre of infinite space.

We lay down in the snow, giving ourselves to the spectacle
first above us, and then towering below
as we hung from the white Earth's curve,
suspended over pulsating light.
Our breath, exhaled and frozen, ice-eye-lashed,
Senses miasma-ed, drawn into the vortex of swirling light.
Words failed me and froze.
It was then, and now, beyond poetry.

Walls

The Mongolian girl at our table
sipped tea, without mares' milk,
surprised at this other way of looking.
The chair she sat on, curiouser and curiouser.
The cups, the curtains, faces in looking glass walls,
landscapes in windows.
"But what are these walls
criss-crossing the plain,
interrupting the gallop of horses,
marking, demarking, tiny prisons of land?"

The boy who sniffs glue, in the shadow of Uluru,
knows, in his bones, always knew,
that the Land owns us, not us the land.
And they sing songs, and sing songlines,
like ancestors bringing the world into being.
Boundaries are notes written in warm orange air,
flaming for an instant and gone,
vaporised water on scarlet earth.
So, what are these fences
interrupting the gallop of horses,
the soundtrack of totem,
the wombat, the wallaby and the kangaroo?
Pinpricks, ice picks in the red heart of the desert...

Clenched hand over clenched fist, walls are rising,
where the graffitied remains of the cold war
wrote itself off in Stasi staccato,
Now, new walls, marking, de-marking.
(Mexico will pay, all men must pay).
Hysteric flags wave in harsh barking winds...
The song of free air is the twitter of iron birds,
the soundtrack, the song-line of untruths.
What is this Wall? What are these walls,
criss-crossing the world,
interrupting the gallop of horses?

Ping Pong with Zoroastrians

Under the Persian wings of Ahura Mazda,
eagle-like over the towers of silence, towers of the wind,
we played ping pong with Zoroastrians
in their temple.
We discussed the eternal war between
Ahura Mazda, Lord of the Light,
and Ahriman, of the dark side,
the principle of evil,
playing out that battle of Light and Darkness
with tiny translucent spheres
and the tap-tap of the bat.

Cello Song

I heard the cello's sad song
where the birds didn't sing, couldn't sing, anymore,
in Sarajevo. Its slow vibrato voice
stepped quavering down the scales
of human suffering, into some dark place
where nothing breathes.
The quick staccato beat of intermittent rapid fire
its only orchestra, echoing like stuttering choruses
against the high blocks of the frightened city.

Invisible listeners in those walls
noted the tremulous adagio,
infinitely sad, infinitely alone, singing the death of humanity.
And here a battered trumpet, or a half-strung violin
answered from the ruins -
a reedy clarinet, a home-made drum, a heartbeat …
uttered a stumbling note, a bar, a phrase:
"While music speaks, there may still be hope …"
"Forget your armaments, your instruments of death
and hear the still small voice of calm …"
that still small cello voice
drifting through gunfire.

Will that lone cello sing now, across the world?

Postcard From the Future

Dear Mankind,

I'm sorry to say this, but I am having a lovely rest and a holiday away from you. Yes, while you are all safely locked away in self-isolation, I am beginning to recuperate. It could take me some time to recover fully, breathe properly again, and glow vibrant blue and green in space once more, with my white swirling luminous clouds, like skirts around me.

You have abused me, my generous resources, my oceans and rivers, mountains and forests too long. You have destroyed my infinite variety of species, with your gas-guzzling multi-national addictions to your own wealth. I warned you. I sent storms over your polluted cities. I sent wildfires through decimated rainforests. I melted ice caps and raised my sea levels. I thought the recent plague of LOCUSTS would send a Biblical message across your horizons…nice touch, as despite all your enormities of greed and corruption, you persist in believing in god, or gods, based on your own insignificant selves.

But you never believed in Me, though I am long-suffering, beneficent and beautiful. Me - your Garden of Eden, your Planet Earth, your habitable Universe. You must believe in me now. Regretfully, I have sent a VIRUS, a plague, a final warning to pull back from the brink and let me breathe again. You have trashed me, exploited me, destroyed my 'endless forms most beautiful and most wonderful.'

So, lock yourselves away, and think. I am not returning to your 'Business as Usual' ever again. I might just shrug you off, like I did with the dinosaurs. I'm having a period of rest and recuperation. A HOLIDAY! I literally wish you WEREN'T here!

Yours Gaia, (Planet Earth)

Landscapes in Colour

Vast RED landscape,
Martian, molten, and marsupialled.
Uluru rears from your subterranean furnace,
burning and luminous at sunset.

Distant BLUE mountains of the Peloponnese,
wine-dark indigo rising from turquoise seas.
Marine blue, haze blue, summer days blue,
or Zeus thunderstorm –hurling charcoal hue.

GREEN Madagascar, mossed and verdigris,
verdant and forested. A million species leap
and crawl through your green entangled abundance
and sing green songs of life.

Dazzling WHITE across the Himalayas of high Tibet,
Everest shoulders the clouds.
Immense presence against the starry night,
sheer charisma in snow form.

YELLOW mountains of China, that fly from afar,
you hold up the palace of the eternal gods,
ochre and pine-parded against the dawn,
then, golden gateway to the evening skies.

PURPLE Pennines, heather tinted moors,
violet-toned in September sun or muted in Northern rains.
Put your moorland arms around me,
my peaty home, my bronze and purple land.

For the love of myths
and history

Ragnarök (the Icelandic End of the World)

Icelanders, huddled in their halls,
felt the earth around erupt in flames,
from ice-rimmed angry mountains, belching smoke.
They saw the liquid blazing road, and Loki's power.
They said, foretold, that all would end in Fire.

As the Fenris-Wolf of howling winter,
padded feral across the frozen fjords' wastes,
they heard the deep chthonic crack like splintering of
subterranean glass.
They sensed Thor's hammer fall again, again,
and pulled thick furs over their pelted heads.
They knew, foretold, that everything would end in Ice.

They sang that when the Fenris-Wolf
leaps from Hel beneath the Ice,
up through the volcano's slavering fiery jaw,
the dark apocalyptic beast will run
in silhouette against Aurora Borealis' undulating sky.
A thousand boiling geysers flare and freeze -
The blazing sun will flicker and turn black -
and then, they told, foretold, in stories round their fires,
the earth would be no more, and all would end,
and everything would end
in Fire and Ice.

Questions

I won a competition with an esoteric prize
- An audience with three random gods:
the bearded one on whirling clouds,
a yellow one with many arms,
and one with many staring eyes.

"You can only ask four questions, so you'd better be
prepared."
I wrote them down religiously,
about the things I cared.
I came into the presence of the Yellow One I'd never heard,
the whirling one with long white beard,
and the one that sat and stared.

"What shape is the wind?" I asked.
"Why are forests green?
Is the moon made of blue cheese?
And what the f**k does everything mean?"

The Old One stroked his long white beard,
arms resting on a passing cloud.
"I have forgotten all I made,
forgotten what "The Word" once said…
I'm old, demented slightly weird.
Don't question me! It's not allowed!"

The Yellow God with many arms,
scratched his yellow head.
At long last he pronounced an "Om!"
and that was all he said.
The Goddess with a hundred eyes,
from a far and distant land,
chanted a long-demented speech
in a high-pitched deafening screech,
in a tongue I didn't understand.

"Time's up, you lucky human!
You've had your theosophic prize.
You'll return uniquely knowledgeable.
You now know the unknowable,
the arcane Truth unshowable...
You are uniquely wise!"

My questions left unanswered,
I'd never learnt the Truth.
But in a Relic Box I took,
a fingernail from the yellow hand,
a cutting from an ancient beard,
an eyelash from a staring eye,
and the fragment of a tooth.

Once home I quickly googled all the questions on my mind.
It answered every one of them...It's easier I find.
But I also built a temple to all gods in the sky.
People venerate the relics,
it's bustling with clerics,
people worship with hysterics.
Oh, I'd love to ask them...WHY???

The Library of Babel – Decoding the Secrets of the Universe

"The Universe, which others call The Library, is composed of an indefinite, and perhaps infinite, number of hexagonal galleries….and from any of the hexagons one can see interminably, the upper and lower floors" Jorges Luis Borges

It was déjà vu.
I had been here before
and I recognised the burnished mirrors
reflecting glass gallery after gallery through glass ceilings
and glass floors.
They were filled with all the volumes ever written.
I had played on the rickety spiral stairways
leading upwards forever in Escher-like arcs.
I had swung down the endless stairwells,
chasing my sisters through the fusty maze,
soaring or sinking into diminishing facets
of the infinite pyramidical structure.
We knew our way around the labyrinth,
without even a silver ball of thread.

We were the daughters of The Librarian.
Where was our mother if not in some metaphysical kitchen
far below, or in some blowzy bed in the Crimson Hexagon?
We laughed at the fusty old men
disputing over the 25 orthographical symbols, the number of shelves,
the number of languages, etc. etc. in the Library of Babel.
"Bla bla bla*" we mimicked, kicking up paradoxes with our feet.
We hid when the 'searchers' threw infidels down stairwells
into the dark voids of the infinite honeycombs
of linguistical mysteries.
We parroted the arcane hieroglyphs in lisps and whispers.
We were fluent in absurdity and cryptographs.

How had I got back in The Library? Was I drawn in by some dream?
Or lured by algorithms of allegories?
Kidnapped perhaps by at the looking-glass spectacled decoders,
and left to count and stamp the inner leaves of limitless volumes?
I heard the door far above me shut with an echoing clang, and a bolt drawn across.
Finality.
I knew I was alone, with no exit. No ladders.
Maybe inside the Cyclical Book itself, curled round me like a serpent.
I might need some time.
Dhcmrlchtdj…?**
Ah well. It all needed a woman's touch,
some clarity, and frankly, a feather duster…
a grand fustian dust-up and declutter…
Oh, and the books need recycling, and digitalising…

*M.L. observes that Bla-Bla-Bla is in fact itself a language.
**A reference to the gobbledegook of Bla-Bla-Bla. Disputed by scholars. It is in fact the secret of the Universe, in code. (ML)

Alternative Histories: Making History a Bit Nicer

1) Harald's eye
The arrow flew but missed.
Harald wrenched it from his horse's bridle.
"That could have taken your eye out!" said his mother.
"Doesn't bear thinking about…"
"It could have changed History" said Harald,
lightly plumping the cushions on his throne.
William slunk back to Normandy and oblivion.

2) No head for figures
"Catholicism out? Not a problem!" said Charles.
"Where do I sign? Oh, and I apologise about those taxes.
I've got no head for figures."
He signed the bottom line, just above the small print
about Beheadings and Civil War.
"There. That should keep the Roundheads happy!" he said,
glancing round the library, where history was already
being re-written.

3) Let them eat cake
"Let them eat cake!" suggested Marie Antoinette.
"Brilliant idea!" exclaimed all the ministers.
So, cakes were ordered throughout France,
and they went down very well with the peasants.
The radical far left loved the fruitcake,
the gentry preferred fairy cakes, but the poor went mad for the
trifles.
No need at all for a revolution.

4) Half a league…
"Listen men. When I give the order to charge,
I want you to get up on yer 'orse and give it some welly.
No mincing about and trotting. No rearing and posing
for equestrian bloody portraits!

I want you to go half a league, only half a league and not a
step further
and then I want you turn round and gallop back here.
We want to make a show, not a bloody massacre.
Tennyson crossed out his jottings, and wrote
'Very little drama to write about on the Crimean front…"

5) Drive –about.
Franz Ferdinand looked at the mirror.
What a time they'd had at the diplomatic ball last night!
He'd had one too many. He didn't look well.
"Cancel that Sarajevo drive-about thing!" He ordered his valet.
"We can do it tomorrow." Gavrilo Princeps had gone home.
 20 million people lived,
 and no trenches were dug anywhere.

6) No blister plasters
Mao's Long March came to a sudden halt when Mao
exclaimed,
"Oooh my feet are killing me!
Did anyone remember to bring the blister plasters?"
No one had, and Mao refused to go another step.
The doctor advised against marching or leaping of any sort,
so, the Great Leap Forward was cancelled.
Mao checked in to a comfy hotel and put his feet up
with Tang Dynasty Poetry, so the Cultural Revolution never
took off.

7) No balls at all
"Herr Hitler…the results of your testicular cancer test are back.
Bad news. We've already had to remove one testicle as you
know.
But now the other one has advanced carcinoma as well.
Sit down, Adolf, if I might call you that… It's terminal, I fear.
We do have palliative care and counselling.
Oh… but you may have to cancel that war."

After Homer: A New Odysseus - Mandela.

This is an epic, but no myths, no legends, and no gods.
It is the story of one man, imprisoned on an island,
a bare cell, marooned in a shark-jailored ocean.
It lay within view of skyscrapers and shopping malls,
and a huge flat-topped mountain.
There modern wanderers could look down
across the tiny wasteland, pitted by pickaxes,
and criss-crossed with high prison wires.

This is a man who could have no hope –
no whispering goddesses urging against despair-
no interventions of bronzed winged warriors,
no magic tricks, or divine committees
on mountain tops. No Pantheistic dreams.
Just one tiny Big Idea.
A thin torch beam in the shadows of night.
The dull black and white, and grey, of apartheid
were his only Helios sunrise
across the vinegar-dark waters.
But he carried the spark, cradled on a dark stalk
inside.

Just as Prometheus, burglar of the Gods,
crept from Mount Olympus with stolen fire
on a fennel stalk, through the shadows
of the lower world,
to help his hand- pottered mortals made of clay,
and bring sparks to scatter in tiny filaments
so dispersed, so disparate as to confuse
the Cloud-Gatherers wrath….

So too this man, unseen,
pulsed miniscule particles of nano-hope, nano-light
across the World from his dark island cell
with his dry fennel-stalk dream.

Totem Song of the Northwest

Eagle soared up on huge wings
and looked down at Creation. His forests invaded,
cut down, his people destroyed.
His tears fell from sky in dark rain,
and he sang his Eagle Song.

Beaver heard Eagle's song
and paused on his river dam.
Saw his rivers colonised and clogged,
his tribes scattered.
His tears fell in rushing waters, and he sang his Beaver Song.

Wolf heard Beaver's Song
and paused. Blood on his trails,
blood on his tracks, fur rent from bone,
cages of iron clamped hard and harsh.
He howled to Moon, and Moon looked down
and saw blood on the mountains.

Salmon and Whale heard Moon
as she drew the tides whispering, back and forth
across Creation.
Salmon leapt, Whale sang
in harmony with Moon and Eagle, Beaver and Wolf.
Then Bear woke from Winter dreams.
"Who dares this?" he growled to Sky.
"Who plunders my creatures of fur and fire?
Who dares?" But a gunshot finished the question.
Bear hibernates now forever.

Then all sang together to Moon and Sun,
but nobody heard as their powers were done.
Nobody heard, for the piercing sound
of the sawing of trees as their world was hacked down.
And today, you can listen as hard as you please

You may hear a wisp
of a whisper of song…
carried along…
and away on the breeze.

Branwen the Raven

Glossy white feathers
catch emerald iridescence from the Sun
as she soars over London.
White raven spirit, Branwen, goddess of love,
is summoned, unlocked, from the Celtic underworld,
by her new-named namesake, the little Raven-girl.
She alights on the White Tower.
Her brother Bran's head was buried far below,
beneath the White Mound, in Bronze age legend,
to keep dead-eyed watch over all Britain.

Now, in soft-plumed fluttering
Branwen flies down to her dark Raven-child,
strokes her glossy down, her midnight feathers,
and the small keen beak, not yet come into its full 'Caw'.
The little eyes blink at her radiance.
Her power transmits.
Rightfully named among ravens, little Branwen,
night-winged spirit of the forest, descended
down through the Mabinogion,
will watch over London
out-blinking Domesday.

Medusa, Set in Stone

Eye, Medusa, Eye-sssss…
upside down in the Waterworks of Byzantium, the Basilica
Cistern.
Insult! Iconoclasm! I, beautiful once,
till that jealous bitch Athene cast me as instantaneous sculptor
petrifying all into statues with my evil eye and my dark looks.
Sssss, if looks could kill, they did.

I Medusa, stone witch, setter in stone, sssss… reduced now
to a Ceiling Gazer - a Vault Voyeur - a Gorgon Goggler!
From my granite neck, Pegasus the flying horse, soared
upwards.
Now a column holding up the dripping vaults of this underworld
is all that leaps from me. Worse than the Caryatids!
Upended, column base. Base! I, Medusa?! Sssss…

Come Perseus, come to me with your magic mirror.
Melt me back into green writhing flesh.
I long to look at you and feel love at… second sight. Sssss…
I didn't choose to freeze to sculptured marble
All those I fixed with my stony gaze. Sssss
I didn't opt for malevolence. Sssss!

It was carved into my soul by marble-eyed Athena. (sigh)
So now I gaze upended, blank faced
at the vast enduring vaults that hold up Byzantium.
My gaze forever set in stone. Eyes, Medusa! Eyes! Sssss…

*Note: Just a stone's throw from Hagia Sophia in Istanbul, you can go
down 53 steps into the enchanted space of the Basilica Cistern built
by the Romans and extended by Justinian. It is a vast vaulted
waterworks, held up by 336 columns. One of these has a strange
base, the huge, inverted image of Medusa. She was once a beautiful
girl, but Poseidon raped her very tactlessly in the Temple of Athene.
There was trouble ahead.*

The Lion Statuette, 40,000 years BC
(Carved out of mammoth tusk)

Someone tamed you
in a flickering cave by the dark half-light of a fire
from the tusk of a ferocious beast,
stalking the neolithic night.
Tap tap tap into a talisman.

Tap tap. Patiently the flint
felt out your contours in the hard tusk.
- the feral jaw and parded jowl,
the furred soft underbelly
curved towards the fatal blow
of some pelt-loined hunter.

Leo erectus,
standing bone, standing tall
in a human hand - God of Beasts-
spirit of an ancient pride,
proud and leonine.
Were you just a bone-toy to a stone-age child?

King Arthur Wakes

Long, long he lay under that hill,
that mighty mythic mountain,
ossified in stone and rock.
Sometimes a breath, a resonance, a breeze
seemed to animate his graphite dreams,
and he slightly stirred, moving his arm to his sleeping sword
in its hilt, as if his time had come:
The prophecy that he would rise when his country was in
need.

Vikings nearly, almost woke him,
piercing the skyline with their beaked warships.
Burning monasteries and beleaguering the North
with their own version of northerness,
ice-hearted halls of darkness and fire.
But Arthur just murmured and slept on.

There were the times too when Plantagenet kings
plundered the people and pillaged the coffers.
Or made poetry their stolen provenance,
stolen from Provence and the Welsh,
to mythologise their power and give it grace.
Arthur almost woke then, as castles rose, and towns burned,
the Welsh undermined; the Scots hammered.

The sleeping stone king twitched, and sat up, shouting "WAR!"
But turned with a marbled snore and slept on.
The Civil War? Surely, he would wake now.
But he dreamt it all, taking no sides.
His England torn. His round table shattered.
But he wept himself back to sleep,
slumbering through his ripped and rended Albion.

He slept well through the Hanoverians,
though he liked not their language.

Empire and Albion, strange bedfellows.
He slumbered through the strait-laced Victorians,
wondering at Tennyson and his Arthurian fame.
He seemed to smile at that Lady of the Lake,
stirring at the memory of that milky arm
raising Excalibur in the dawn of his time.

Until World War 1 woke him from deep REM.
He flinched at the trenches,
and the moustachioed generals,
false knights charging into the Valley of Death
with a false Grail.

He dreamt on too, through World War 2,
confused as with a half awakening nightmare
of Hitler and Himmler
plundering - again - 'plunder' - his myth of the Round Table.
"False! False!" he shouted,
forcing blood to course into his stone lips.
"Not in my name the Shoah, the shame, the wreck of nations!"
He wished himself out of that dream, into a new dream of
Europe.

But war rumbled underground,
shaking the earth.
He feels the tremors visceral, in his granite gut,
deep inside that forgotten hill.
Stalactites crack. Rocks crash down. Albion falls.
The last of all wars…
Landscapes burn and seas rise. Nations erupt in fire.
Pan-global nuclear war. Skylines immolate in flashes.
A sudden crash of catastrophe. Pause. Ear-splitting silence.

Arthur wakes, sitting bolt upright, reaches for Excalibur.
He totters wildly on stone legs and strikes the cave door.
"I am ready to save the world. It is time! I have come!"
He strides, silhouetted against ruined cities and heaving skies,

and the topless tower blocks, stickle-backed as skeletons.
"I have come! I have woken!"
But he speaks to silence. Excalibur wavers in monoxide air.
A long aeon of silence.
Arthur has come. But the world is gone…

The Horses of Byzantium

Lente lente currite noctis equi...
We have paced and strutted
chariotless through the ages
from distant Byzantium with its cheering crowds
and its stadium of billowing red and green silk flags.
We snorted our bronze nostrils at Theodora herself,
the wily philosopher-dancer who stole Justinian's heart
and shared his throne.

Our fetlocks and flanks sweated copper,
as our side-stepping motionless advance
took us through centuries of orthodoxy and power.
We trotted on, untrammelled, while icons were crushed and
burned,
we were beyond iconic, beyond imagination,
pure animal energy, burnished in bronze.

Then they came. The Doge Dandalo and his 4th Crusaders,
those thieving Venetians, seeking treasure,
sacking the Towers of Byzantium.
They came for us, uprooting our copper hooves, tore us from
our reins.
We were thrown in a ship, where we sprawled like discarded
fragments
while white foam horses sped us across wide waters, to
Venice.
Then, sacrilege: They heaved us on to their Basilica

To be their Victory, their stolen glory.
They are rulers of the seas. We move their invisible chariots of
power.
Our heads face East in longing for lost Byzantium...
But lente lente, the time is coming
when Venice sinks beneath the waves,
and we shall gallop free, horses of the sea, horses of the night.

Shakespeare's Villains, on the Touchy Subject of Remorse

(In conniving couplets)

Macbeth:
Ok, I murdered Duncan. T'was the wife's idea.
She is the one who is to blame, I fear.
I did regret she'd done it, yes of course.
- But only felt *vicarious* remorse!

Richard the Third:
I stacked up bodies both in barrels and towers.
My body-count could barely fit 3 hours!
Remorse? Do I, 'who was not made for dalliance,' feel *remorse?*
Not likely! Meanwhile…'A horse! My kingdom for a horse!'

Claudius:
Yes, I poured poison in the ear of Hamlet's dad.
An act of fratricide that made me… almost… sad.
Remorse for *regicide?* Well, no, but some remorse
for hours of naval gazing by that fool, Hamlet, of course!

Regan and Cornwall:
Expect us to show remorse for Gloucester's rheumy eyes?
- mere dramatic device - vile jellified surprise!
We didn't need to kill that poor sod Lear…
He was mad beyond his sell-by date, we fear.

Brutus:
"Et tu, Brute?" Brutus, even you?
OK, I take responsibility for the action of the few.
Regret, that Shakespeare wrote such murderous scenes.
Remorse, that ends don't justify the means.

Iago:
You ask me if I have one small regret in life

for making Othello mad enough to kill his lovely wife?
His jealous rages reaped their own rewards!
Can Shakespeare say the pen is mightier than *whispered*
words?

Moral:
Shakespeare's villains show but scant remorse
when interviewed on homicides we *saw* them do, of course.
Hanging's too good for them, or damp and padded cell.
So, let's consign them to a post-dramatic, post-*traumatic,*
literary… hell!

At the Existentialist Café with Apricot Cocktails

At the Existentialist Café
in an old, converted mill,
some wannabe philosophers met
to discuss Life, Death and Free Will.

We sipped on apricot cocktails,
and nibbled Yorkshire pies,
till the ghosts of past philosophers
arose before our eyes.

There was Plato burbling on and on
about some damp old cave,
while Diogenes blubbed from his Cynic tub
that all Mankind's a slave.

Epicurus was in dispute
with three post-Christian thinkers,
saying that gods are not involved
and Theists are all blinkered.

Then up rose Aristotle
with his arm round Thomas Aquinas,
and sang in perfect harmony
to entertain us diners.

Berkeley blew bubbles from a jar,
Schopenhauer didn't demur,
while Jean-Paul Sartre embraced Descartes
and thought, therefore they *were.*

Heidegger arrived at phenomenal speed,
at Husserl's express request
to question what *is* it that we are?
… and whose idea was best?

That caused a philosophic furor,
Hume, fuming, joined the fight.
Rousseau weighed in with the Rights of Man,
and Socrates questioned what *was* right.

Nietzsche was praising the prescience of power,
but Chomsky was not convinced.
Then Machiavelli got a knife in his belly
from a powerful passing prince.

We swilled our cocktails down in haste,
our unpaid bill refuting.
We left the philosophers to pay,
which led to *more* endless disputing!

Human Racehorses

"What do you do?" I asked the Australian lady politely.
"Human racehorses," she replied,
and went on to explain in great detail
about people - management, job opportunities and
government-sponsored back-to-work initiatives.

But I wasn't listening. Human racehorses?
I was seeing steaming centaurs, with fetlocks glistening,
and foam-flecked withers, manes flowing back in the wind,
the thunder of mythical hooves,
galloping with silk flags streaming
on ancient turf, over some Grecian Beecher's Brook
in distant Olympia.

She was explaining, meanwhile, how human racehorses
were entering a new phase and were often outsourced.
There were opportunities for go-ahead people,
like herself, in IT Management.

But I was hearing the roar of cheering crowds
of Titans and Minotaurs, and the elderly mentor centaurs
like Chiron, as the man-part of the centaurs,
dressed in silk-striped racing colours
urged on by their beast-halves with urgent whips and hoarse
cries,
towards the finishing post.
Nymphs and satyrs were already hurrying to the totes and
bookies
with the winning tickets...

But she had just finished her finishing line,
"Yeah, I'm really enjoying Human Racehorses"
So, I looked at her blankly and said," Goodness me.
How very... fabulous!"

Mount Olympus

Heavens above! The sheer rearing beauty of it,
with twelve peaks at its summit.
After two days walking upwards through sunlit forests of
dappled green
you are there, among the gods.
Until that moment you forget the Olympians are here,
and that Zeus the sky god jealously patrols the vertiginous
edges,
hurling his bolts down after scattering mortals
in their climbing boots and anoraks -
(with Olympus cameras.)

One forgets that 'picturesque' is not a word in Zeus' terrible
vocabulary.
But 'Hubris' is. He doesn't like to be challenged.
So it was that with 'Hubris' committed, mountain heights
reached,
we leapt lightly down boulder after boulder,
without Promethean foresight.
We heard the Bolt like a drumbeat on Earth.
We felt the mountain tremble.
Birds fell quiet.
Again - a dark chthonic thud
echoing against the forested flanks,
but sounding from the dark stomach of the mountain.

We looked up
and saw a dark cloud colonising the blue skies.
Flashes like the whites of Zeus' eyes
searching for us guilty mortals
who had dared to stare at the home of the Gods.
Again, he stamped his mountain foot,
and the rains fell like a curtain of furious blackness.
We ran and ran, ducking lightning strikes
Like spies trespassing under fire.

67

Even when at last we reached our car
we drove like madmen, past Dion,
where Zeus' sacred altar lies abandoned and thunderstruck,
through tsunamis of punishing rain.
Then, stopped and looked back, to see the silhouetted Olympus
in cymbal clashes of storm. Zeus was raging.

Then on we drove on black shining roads
twisting like a leviathan through hectic sheets of rain,
as luminous as Deucalion's flood,
in the turmoil of headlight and spray, round the vast bay.
We came at last to a distant town called Ouranopolis,
city of the Sky.
There we sat on a balcony in the harbour,
and watched the greatest storm on Earth
rage towards us,
striding the seas like a Colossus,
with firecrackers at its fingers, slashing the firmament,
lashing breakers at its feet, striding after ... Us.

Then, Zeus, unable to spot us in his blind fury,
as we crouched guilty in our third-floor room,
threw a few more thunderbolts across the bay
and left at dawn.

Death, the Stalker (after Emily Dickinson)

Death called me on my landline.
Just four small words he said.
"I'm coming for you!" - That was all
- Then the line went dead.

I sat - dazed - at my laptop
and saw an email there -
from death@demonopenworld -
"I'm coming - so beware!"

I seized my mobile phone - and saw
a terse - unholy - text.
"I'm coming for you -so beware!
I'm coming for you next."

A shadow at my doorway -
a creak upon the stair.
"I'm coming for you - I'm coming!"
I felt his chill breath - on the air.

My heart collapsed - my pulse stopped - dead.
My eyes rolled up in fright.
The silhouette at the doorframe came -
and took me - in the night.

Since then - I've wailed against the winds,
howled at each windowpane.
"Death has stolen my life away! -
Oh! - Let me in again!"

La Mer

Wash over me waves,
in desolate foam.
The tide came in and washed away the tracks of
people, rubbish, lolly sticks in wake of ice-cream men.
London has returned to London with its picnic chairs.
We are alone again.

Deep in shells the sea heart beats,
telling the restless struggle with the vortexed sky.
Debussy is curling over my mind,
slow, organic,
syncopated with the suspirant sigh,
of waves on rocks,
lapping in shallow sand beds
with erosive beat.
… Or blindly fingering, feeling for the shore
with long seaweed.

The Pythia: Priestess of Delphi

A suppliant came,
and in the dark hush of the temple
I was brought, half-drugged with poppy flowers,
and sat astride a tripod, thighs splayed,
across the deep cleft of the earth, where vapours swirled up
from the Omphalos, the visceral stomach of Hades.
I saw my visions there.
"Apollo's lips" I thought, I conjured up,
slumped forward, breathing the numinous narcotic air.
"Talk to me, speak through me, use all of me
to speak your truths.
Whisper to me your arcane prophecies fogged in riddles!"
A madness came across my mind,
a cyclone of thoughts, spreading through brain, arms, fingers,
thighs.
I trembled, I shook with a divine seizure,
Falling sideways across that mouth of the Underworld,
That deep hallucinogenic gash of gaseous steam
where the Python flickers its tongue and speaks.
For there, above me, was the Delphic Temple
now lit with a volcano's fire.
Apollo's face, a golden mask,
with fiery hair, and blazing eyes,
stared down on me and moved his lips,
he spoke in lava tones, fire in his breath:
"Get out of here, you abortion of Nature!
Hells-fury of all the gods' hate!
You rank abomination of Apollo's sacred Oracle!
For you will marry your mother and murder your father!
Be gone!"
And through the seizure that shook me
I whispered what I heard with my last breath,
and died.
But the suppliant ran,
Ran far into the night - and beyond.

Silkie Ascending

A dark glittering is my tale,
flipped and too quick to see,
out of the oil-dark water.
I am Silkie, silver queen
of the seal grey sea,
up from full fathom five
to flop on rocks, sending diamonds flying
over the lap-lapping of waves,
singing my eerie echoing seal-woman song.

I loosen my pelt, my wet speckled fur
and stand wholly woman, naked
under that half rocking
ghost boat of the tilting moon.
Kicking my flippers aside
I flex my toes,
and now with silken fingers
catch the rope rigging
of that twisting ladder to the moon,
and climb from water through earth to air.

I am queen of three elements now, creature of myth,
as I float suspended in the upper ocean of the sky,
on a slither of moonlight for a ship.

History in Blues
(Voidokilia Bay, Messenia, Peloponnese.)

I am speechless, voiceless, wordless at so much blue.
Some designer-God, Hephaistos, the artistic one,
must have leant down with a compass,
and marked its semi-circle,
then painted with a brushstroke,
crushed lapis and turquoise
of the pure sea-glass inside.
I paddle in its swirling skirts,
swimming the landscape with my eyes.

Beyond Voidokilia, Divari Lake with its moonstone waters,
reaches the lapping shore of cobalt blue Navarino Bay,
shadowed with eighty Turkish ghost ships in its indigo depths.
Everywhere the birds are singing
to the blue-grey mountains beyond,
and Nestor's Palace under the cornelian sky.
Singing to the wine dark Navarino and distant Pylos,
and the purple shades of Ottoman sailors.

Singing to the phantom-haunted crags of Sphacteria,
to ruins left by Franks,
and the iridescent sea-horseshoe of Voidokilia.
What else is there to do but sing?
History in blues.

Sun – the Shining One, Comes to Tea

(a tribute to Mayakovsky)

I threw my arms up to the sky,
and shouted to the hidden sun,
"Oh, Shining One, please tell me why
this endless rain is never done
and why you've let the summer fly?"

Sun pushed apart the sheets of clouds,
like curtains on a lit-up stage.
"I'll just step down. I can explain
why all the weather's in a rage…
The whole world's gone insane."

He stepped down to my garden green,
burning with golden fiery rays.
I donned my sunhat and my cream.
The cherry trees lit in a blaze
as in a luminescent dream.

He drank the tea but burnt the toast.
We talked into the starless night.
"I light the world from coast to coast,
but poets too must shine their light,
on all the things they value most."

He sadly wiped his shining eyes,
and said that from his view in Space,
he'd seen the wild tempestuous seas,
and had to blame the Human Race
for being greedy and unwise.

"Come, my poet, let us write,
and shine, across these tattered oceans!
Blaze to the deeps of the last night,
luminous in verse and light,

creating vast commotions."

I gave his arm a little pat,
reminding him why we were sad.
He hadn't shone at all through May,
he'd let the Arctic winds run mad,
and he apologised for that.

We parted as the best of friends
and neighbours too, who love to meet.
Then, as the night's discussion ends,
the Sunrise walked off down the street,
and shone through June to make amends.

Prufrock in Lockdown 2020

Let us go now, you and I,
while Lockdown rains blur the London sky,
through the empty streets hand in hand,
down the now deserted Strand.
A million faces pressed to windowpanes,
their sheen of isolation reflected in the endless rains.

The women in the galleries are strictly social-distanced.
while people kneel before the police in silent masked
resistance.

Is it time? No "Time gentlemen please". Unreal city…
The ghosts of crowds flit through Whitehall with phantom
vanilla lattes,
lives marked out in plastic spoons, tick tock…. Tick tock.
Drizzle turns monuments to a pointillist, pointless, poignant
haze.
Unreal city, slurred to a chiaroscuro fog spreading to a grey
horizon.

Empty museums, banks, shops, all quiet as a tomb.
And should we, as we walk across Waterloo Bridge,
spot one human hunkered under cardboard,
stop and pass the time of day? Drop a coin in a cup?
Is there time to sanitise the helping hand? Is there time?
And should you and I, with strictly six,
gather to picnic in the gaping silence of Trafalgar Square,
just to shout "We are! We are! We ARE here!"
And listen to the trailing echo spin?

The women in the galleries are strictly social-distanced.
While people kneel before the police in silent masked
resistance.

In every room across the globe hungry eyes, hungry fingers

probe phones to join the hectic superhighway of hyper-reality.
We are removing to new dimensions.
We become Indian gods with 12 arms, a hundred digitalised
fingers.
Even love and war are virtual and enhanced.

And what of us who are old, steeped in blues and birdsong?
Can we still hear the roar of lions across Trafalgar Square,
and shout to Nelson on his dizzy pedestal....
"The sea! the sea! Ho Thalassa!"
No. That's not it. Not what I meant at all...

The Emperor Whisperer

I am a slave. The 'Emperor Whisperer'.
My job, my special privileged job, was to stand behind the emperor,
in his chariot at some great triumph in Rome,
whispering sweet nothings of obscenities and insults
into the Imperial Ear, lest 'he' should get 'above himself'.
"You're mortal" I sneered.
"You are not an effing god, you're not becoming one,
you're not even a little bit divine.
In fact, you are a sneaky little twatus, (yes, that IS vulgar Latin)
…a bastard, a bum-boy, a 'pederastus'.

Romans! Lock up your wives! The bald adulterer has come!
This fat git with a face like a Colosseum toilet…"
Well, it worked ok my first two emperors.
They took it on the chin.
Vespasian didn't get above himself till his deathbed.
"I think I AM becoming a god!" were his last words.
Titus built nice columns.
Wasn't a god enough to stop Vesuvius spouting!
It was Domitian who went Awolus. Insanus. Pottyus.
Soon as we stepped out of the chariot after the Triumph,
it was the Mamertine Prison for me,
in chains, with my tongue cut out.
No bloody sense of humour.
He turned out to be a 100 per cent bastardus material.

But now I have been summoned back from the underworld,
My talents as an emperor whisperer have been recognised.
May 9th. Big Parade, a triumph in Scythia.
'Russia' in your vulgar lingo.
A Tsar, apparently… He thinks he's an Emperor old style.
Thinks he's a god like Jupiter.
Unsinkable as a …warship.
My job is to stand behind him as the tanks roll by.

"You're not a God mate.
You're a skunky little Puke-kin, Mr Putin.
A criminal megalomaniac with a low I.Q.,
and a nasty spot of psychosis.
You need locking up for a long, long time, matey,
with your lying tongue fed to the lions.
Or spread-eagled naked on a high Caucasian crag,
with the Russian eagles pecking out your liver… Forever!
(Bastardus!)"

For the love
of Love

s

Geography Lovers

You are my Far East and my Wild West.
Let's map each other out with our hands,
ride over each other's horizons with soft-fingered horsemen,
mark out equatorial regions with a survey of kisses,
trace our coastlines and soft lapping shores.

You are my Polar North and my Deep South.
Let's explore our tropics and equators with our lips.
We'll stretch out our longitudes across wild savannahs,
we'll lay our latitudes across wide shores,
and entangle magnetic poles with our limbs.

Fissures and fumaroles flicker with subterranean fire
along our earth bodies and ocean veins.
Sky and Earth joined.
You are my geography.
I am your map.

Ethical People Smuggler

I will build a ship
from the flotsam that floats in the News.
I will make a sail from rags of empathy
and an engine from outcast fragments
of battered hopes.

I saw them lying in rows,
the drowned ones, drowned with their dreams.
They were herded like non-persons
onto the doomed Titanics.
They were robbed and frisked,
and risked on paper boats
onto the thrashing Mediterranean
like sea-kill and fish-fodder.

I saw too, those who survived,
lurking in bus shelters on Gozo,
or eking out a non- existence
in purgatory huts on Lesbos, or Sicily.
Each one a philosopher, a dreamer, a human.
Each one a novel or poem or story.

I will build a boat, I will build a flotilla,
and haul them from the waves.
I will build an Armada
to wage war on people smugglers,
and their dirty pirate trade.
I will bring those huddled masses
through their darkness and terror,
through storms and blighted Odysseys.
I will steal them to the safety
of friendship, and embraces,
to release them like threatened species
of migrant birds, into the wild possibilities of Europe, to fly.

Ethical People Smuggler?
I can only dream. But in my heart my arms go out,
to pull them aboard my bright ship,
from the unfolding, heaving dark waters
of this global maelstrom.

Two Armchairs on a Hebridean Beach

A local bus runs once a day
to the isolated village, facing the Atlantic.
A phone box and a few grey houses.
A kirk, and beyond that, within a mile's wander,
stretches a white beach
running to a headland, a mountain,
where golden eagles command the coast with surveillance
eyes,
watching land and sky.

Gentle seals, paddle the waters,
singing haunting songs, "join us in the waves.
We are wild, we are waiting."
Deserted sands, soft, hospitable.
Distant hills, blue, hazy and heat misted.
Gulls calling, scent of ozone and heather,
hinting long tented nights under Hebridean skies.

And there, bizarre as an elephant in a blue room,
or a parlour al fresco in a blue horizon,
sat two armchairs, upholstered, velveted, inviting,
tilted at a quizzical angle … alluring.
A-skewed Canutes, we sat tranced in them for a week
and missed our boat back, and beyond that, our train home.
I think perhaps…forever.

.

Early Spring

The rhododendrons felt it in their sap.
"Spring" they thought, but it was January.
They filled and budded, fat and sleek,
their furled red petals
showing like veins behind the green carapace
of their smooth beetle-bodied buds.

Snow came in February,
and they hesitated, unsure.
One brave bud teetered on the brink of flowering
and was frost -bitten instantly by winter's icy tooth.
The rest held back, fertility on hold,
retracting back into their pangolin leaved husks.

March suffused in with a breathless outburst
of sunshine and yellow.
The rhododendrons are sulking now.
They know the trick.
They're not showing their crimson faces
till May.

Archaeology of Self

Never clear out your attic
or clean your decades of accumulated strata.
You are your own Troy,
layer by layer, built up in carbon,
tiered high as Babylon laid low as Persepolis.
You are traceable only by fragments
and filaments of dirt left by your footprints
on unwritten history.
Your drawers hold the tenderest fragments
of coincidence, conflicts, collaborations, joys.
Your cupboards flow like tides and waterfalls
through your silted existence,
bearing the detritus of your dreams
like bobbing half-glimpsed treasures
disappearing from view as soon as remembered.
You are your own museum!
And those books, other peoples' voices,
entwined with yours from childhood. Save them.
Even those poor unread books may call you yet
from the dustied archives of your bookshelves.
Oh, keep them all. They are your Nazca lines,
your neolithic cart-tracks, mapping your existence
from life into an abrupt ocean.

The Old Bed

Yes, it had to go,
too sagged and loose-springed now. I hit the ceiling
when he, partner of living and night-time dreams,
sat down heavily after some dawn lavatory raid,
or late-night insomniac wander.
The end of an era, the end of a bed of 40-odd years.
It lasted almost a marriage in the front line.
It held cocooned the tenderest passions
of pure red joys,
not a witness, but a conspirator in love.
Always haloed and glowing in warm light
with shadow arms of orange, crimson gold,
it embraced us, embracing in its springed embrace.
This marriage bed, the inner hub,
has like John Donne's bed
been centre of the universe to our wandering planets.

We have travelled, transported in its magic carpet surface
over continents and time,
through myth, history and legend,
through poetry and novels.
It has been our comfy library–ship of dreams
to bookish pleasures.
This bed too, this old bed,
has been a warm red nest to children and grandchildren,
padding on little feet to shelter in its harbour,
to be comforted, held close and read to.
Breakfast in bed, coffee in bed, books in bed,
bliss in bed, children early morning.
"Swap parents!" they would shout,
and run to the other side.

Too squashy, too springless and worn-out
by all the life lived in it, on it, -
This old bed, this dream-boat bed, must go

into bed history, into bed heaven or hell
where all beds end.
Into the skip, already in pieces.
It is junk in a junk-heap, it is history.
Gone over our horizon
into eternal night.
Rest in peace. Sweet dreams, dear Bed.

Inner Landscapes

In Lockdown, withdrawn from the wider landscapes of reality
I always yearned to travel,
I have explored, instead, the inner landscapes
of memory, dreams, reflection.
The faraway caverns, stalactited, stalacmited,
of memory, with deep recesses
leading inwards and downwards to complex hidden tunnels
and dark places to light up with luminous torches.
Or climb the great towering mountain ranges of dreams
with all the vertigos of life lived too hopefully, optimistically.

Then, the forests of dark fears, and the almost floating
woodlands
of childhood, with its flying carpets of bluebells,
and embroidery of lichen-brightness recalled through snatched
music.
Small touchstones in the maze, patterns in the walls,
press open entrances to forgotten portals…
or sudden underground passages once explored, grown over.

I love this vast National Park inside my head.
Sifting the sands, skimming whole ranges of my imagination
on mind-skis, on snowshoes,
in baskets of hot-air memory balloons,
or grappling irons to climb karst pinnacles.

But oh, the upkeep of the older mind!
The estate-managing of inner thought!
The gilley-control of the ranging hills,
The rampant overgrown woodlands now beyond control.
I must rebuild now, stone by stone, the fallen walls,
collect the cracked jigsaw pieces,
remove the wind-blown fleeces on the fences,
clear the neural pathways choked with moss,
and weeds of doubt and failing connections.

Shore up the will to go back out, return, engage.

The overgrown lanes all lead inwards to the maze.
I must re-tarmac, now. Forge new highways.
Upgrade my inner broadband.
Lay new drains, and culverts.
Sharpen my diggers, my mental JCBs.
Wheel in cranes, rebuild, remake, rediscover
the gritty Pennines of real life.

Sekhmet, a Talisman

My granddaughter brought me Sekhmet
Lion-headed goddess, all the way from Egypt,
bubble-wrapped in a Christmas bag.

She, who is all powerful,
Mistress of Dread
Goddess of War and Plague,
Daughter of Ptar, the primal breath,
one who Evil trembles before,
she who breathes desert fire to defeat enemies,
she who turned the Nile red with human blood.
And she who exhales plagues upon the lands and peoples.
Ra, the sun god, had to pacify her lion-like wrath
by offering her beer dyed with vermillion red
to quench her blood lust.
She became so drunk, so intoxicated
that she vowed peace, protection and healing
to her friends, (but not to her enemies.)
Now, this drunken leonine lass
holds Festivals of Intoxication
in the 'Porches of Drunkenness' in Luxor.

I ask you, is this a suitable present for a Granny?
My house is wrecked with nightly warfare... broken crockery,
furniture overturned.
The garden is trashed, the lawn's turned red. Bottles strewn
everywhere.
I am covered with boils and buboes...while she sits on my
mantlepiece
as a tame as a domesticated cat on a grandmother's lap.
Nice puss. Sweet Pusskins.
Here's beer in your bowl.

Franklin's Song

"*T'was homeward bound one night on the deep,*
Swinging in my hammock I fell asleep.
I dreamed a dream and I thought it true..."
the redheaded girl sang on that shore of Beechey Island
where long ago Franklin had wintered.
At her feet lay rusty tins among the pebbles
as though Franklin's men had only just thrown them down,
poisoned by lead, debilitated by cold.

"*On Baffin's Bay where the whale fishes blow,*
The fate of Franklin no man may know..."
Franklin looked out over the groaning vastness of ice.
"We must wait till spring opens up the ocean once more
and we can map a route to the Northwest Passage I know lies
beyond.
No choice." But his voice was lost to the deep growl of the
frozen sea.

"*Their ship on mountains of ice was drove...*" sang the
redhead girl.
"*Only the eskimo in his skin canoe*
was the only one who ever got through..."
She gazed across the surreal landscape of lost history.
Expedition after expedition had been sent to find them.
"*Ten thousand pounds would I truly give*
To find on earth that my Franklin doth live" she sang to the
desolate winds.

Now, a group of schoolchildren had come exploring so
effortlessly,
by plane and boat to the place where explorers met death.
They too were gripped by that primal urge to discover new
horizons.
It was in her, it was her dream too.
She was part of Franklin's dream,

It had led her to this haunted sailor place,
this romantic desolation of unknown fate.
The song and the story had transfixed her in its ice and
mystery.
That sweet sad Pentangle song I had sung to my daughter,
had penetrated its magisterial grace notes into her soul
forever.
The power of song. The aching power of song.

*Lyrics from original song, "Lady Franklin's Lament" circa
1850.

Note: 10 years after my daughter's journey to Arctic Canada I found myself telling John Renbourne,(who sang the song on the Pentangle Concert I had been to in 1968), about my daughter singing Franklin's song on the beach of Beechey Island. He was very touched. 30 years later I discovered that the wreck of Franklin's ship, Erebus, was found in 2014. And while visiting Vancouver Maritime Museum in 2016, we found that the other ship, Terror, had just been discovered, coincidentally, in Terror Bay at Nunavut.

Diana's Garden

Stepping through a door in the wall
through to the secret garden,
I enter the still, explosive kaleidoscope of Diana's studio,
a garden of painting,
leading to a garden -
a world within a world, like a shrine sacred and silent,
which burns like a crucible of fire and colour,
radiating from its centre, outwards.

Now, I am alone in someone's head,
hearing the quickening pulse,
sensing the orchestras of shape and pigment tuning around
me.
The sheer untrammelled joy of colour
flashing from garden to darkened studio,
rioting across walls and canvasses
like wildfire at midnight.
This is the presence of creativity not found in galleries.
This is vivid, raw and wild -
indefatigable and irrepressible.

This is life force in a small tight space,
pressed down and running over.
This is the secret of Diana's secret garden, her studio:
It is full of visions.

For my friend and inspiration, Diana Henderson, who died in 2022,
and who painted the cover of this collection.

The Mother

If I died now, I think I would return
on still summer nights to my garden.
I'd wander out from darkness quietly up the path,
and stop to stroke the ghosts of my two cats
as they sit sunning themselves in the moonlight.
If you looked out, you'd see the pale glow of my dress,
and hear me humming softly, preoccupied with gathering
flowers out of the vibrant night
for some vase in the hushed gloom of a cold church.
But when the winds blow from the moors,
and rain lashes the trees against the house,
or fierce November howls beneath the doors,
you'll see me pressed against the windowpane
with blazing eyes and streaming hair,
calling to see my children once again.
Fists noiseless on the glass,
cries voiceless in the storm.
Then let me in, please let me in,
and welcome home the cruelly exiled ghost!

Moon Breath

May Moon, Full Flower Moon,
serene and haloed,
so close I can feel your silver breath,
breathe down on us
and fill us with moonlight.
Rein back the white mares of the tides.
Blow soft on the warming oceans,
rippling, ruffling the surface with fractured reflections.

Guardian Moon, Blood-Moon rising,
flushed and breath-taking on crimson mists,
you oversee Earth
from your sky-high journey.
We are burnt out, airless, breathless and stricken.
Breathe down on us. Disperse this miasma!
Exhale your luminous calm,
and fill us with moonlight.

Snow

Holed up in snow,
hedgehog-souled,
curled back-to-back
in our warm red bed.

Outside a stark whiteness.
A soft white silence
dove-feathers our crimson nest.
No need to go out.

Hibernate, and let the snowflakes
white wall us within.

Goldfinch Child

A Goldfinch came and sang to me
from our little apple tree.
"Where is she, the Goldfinch Child?
Where is Djenna? Where is she?"

I whistled softly piping words
in the Language of the Birds,
"Djenna will return again
to love each Goldfinch, Robin, Wren.

But times have altered, time moves on.
Djenna sings a different song,
caged in a plagued city far away.
She'll come and sing another day."

Darker times will fade, must pass.
My Goldfinch will return at last,
run through the garden, free and wild -
My darling little Goldfinch Child!

*For my granddaughter and all children locked in tiny flats during
lockdown, 2020, and their grandparents who miss them.*

The Window

I remember a window long ago
opening out on a summer evening
on to a garden of peonies and lavender.
My sister and I leant out to listen
to our grandmother, white haired and beautiful,
playing Chopin in the room downstairs,
pouring the sounds from her rippling hands
out into the vibrant evening air -
music sent and received through windows.
And when we slept, we dreamed
in chords and arpeggios of liquid light.

The Box of Delights

I opened a book, a Pandora's box of delights,
spiralling upwards and outwards to new worlds.
The wolves are running. I feel my hair stand up on end.
I am wolf … I am cat, I am whom I want.
I am the glittering girl on a black mare with gold wings
I enter an ancient picture frame to meet the great great
grandfather,
and travel to other worlds, long ago, aboard the Plunderer,
and just make it home in time for tea.
I am with Kay, my boy soulmate.
We slide along corridors disguised as mice,
follow Herne the Hunter bounding through forests
on his sleigh drawn by unicorns.
I wear scarlet shoes to jump over water.
I meet the Punch and Judy man, holding arcane secrets of
magical power,
the Box of Delights.
I am transported, terrified, to the Wizard Abner Brown,
encounter Sylvia Pouncer, my first brush with evil, governess
turned bad.
Transmogrified, we sing with mermaids.
And always, the wolves are running, running, running.
My hair billowing behind me, I must fly back inside my bed,
heart racing,
and turn the torch off, beneath the bedclothes,
before Sylvia Daisy Pouncer turns me back
into a real child.

It's Gone: The Inner Landscape of Dementia

I was once in this place…where was it now?
Things weren't so blurred then,
there were timetables and special days.
There were gardens with little walls… apple tree games.
People talked with you not at you….
I remember once…no, …it's gone…
A kind woman who held my hand,
and I had pigtails and a smocked dress.
Who was it once kissed me?
No, it's misted up…I felt it, but it's… gone.

I am here now,
Walled up in my own country.
The walls are indistinct and jigsawed.
A hand comes at me with a plate
and a sudden noise of clapping startles me,
from a black box that never opens.
Boxes open, don't they?

That reminds me… no, it's… gone…
There was music, a sort of song.
I can dance to it, arms in the air
suspended as I am in slow swirling ether
the colour of lavender.
I can smell the lavender…
I tap my feet, but the melody drifts apart,
un-focusses, disintegrates
just when I almost touched it… it's gone.

There was a man, with a loving voice
who held me… No… No…he's gone…
A flickering black and white world
where we kissed, and he said… something…
Something… gone…
I almost grasped it, but it's… gone.

"Get your hands off me!"
"Let me go!"
Rough hands pin me down.
I am bustled up in a white nappy, legs forced apart.
Someone says, "Calm down Freda!"
But they aren't kind, I can tell.
I shout to those outside the wall.
They are sitting in chairs, the blank staring women.
But they are gone, quite…gone.
There was somebody. There was something…
But it's… gone.
It's gone.

Songs from Story of the Earth

Songs written for "The Story of the Earth", and interactive performance and puppetry project for children

The Insects' Song

Out of sparks of flame and fire
We whispering warriors came.
Too colourful to catalogue,
Too numerous to name.

Like tiny intricate machines
We fizz and buzz on filigree wings
About the planet's business,
Armed with darts and stings.

We scuttle with armoured carapace
On armoured plated legs
About the planet's business
Laying potent insect eggs.

Flamboyant wings and fluttering flight
Jewelled creatures of the light-
Dragonflies and butterflies,
Soft moths whose business is the night.

The Bird Song

We caught our song from the music of the spheres,
And now we sing it to the Earth, in jungle, forest and echoing
woodland,

Chorus:
A million tiny voices swell,
The story of the Earth to tell -
Diversity and harmony,
Diversity and harmony.

We sing the ancient songline of a million years,
To the wide eternal sea, river, lake and frozen waste,

Chorus:
A million tiny voices swell,
The story of the Earth to tell -
Diversity and harmony,
Diversity and harmony.

We weave our many-coloured strands of song
Into a rainbow of living sound - A symphony of life on Earth,

Final Chorus:
A million tiny voices swell,
The story of the Earth to tell -
Diversity and harmony,
A million tiny voices swell,
The story of the Earth to tell -
Diversity and harmony,
Diversity and harmony.

Bio-Diversity Hoe Down

Chorus:
Bow to your partners, sniff and sniff again,
Only eat him up if he's lower in the food chain!
Mark out your territory, yer habitat-tat.
Survival of the fittest means you've got to adapt!

Some of us grew stripes and some of us grew spots
Some of us grew patterns and polka dots.
Some of us made smells like the smelly old skunk,
One grew a snout, and another grew a trunk.

Chorus:
Bow to your partners, sniff and sniff again,
Only eat him up if he's lower in the food chain!
Mark out your territory, yer habitat-tat.
Survival of the fittest means you've got to adapt!

Some of us grew antlers to clatter and to clash
Horns to batter, or tails to thrash
We can kick and bite or suck or sting-
We can snarl and growl... and some of us can sing!

Chorus:
Bow to your partners, sniff and sniff again,
Only eat him up if he's lower in the food chain!
Mark out your territory, your habitat-tat.
Survival of the fittest means you've got to adapt!

An Ice Age comes, and our fur grows thick,
And when the ice melts, we learn to swim quick.
We've adapted so much and diversified so long,
Why, we're even adapting as we sing this song!

The Reptile Song

Unblinking eye
Unthinking brain
Chthonic soul, evolving from the living rock we came.
Cold-blooded, thin
With hooded skin.
Pachyderm and prehistoric predators, the sea and land we
claim
Unassuming
Slow consuming,
Time devours all but our reptilian hold upon the ancient earth.

Also by the author

Poems included in "In the Company of Poets" - Holme Valley
Poets
… and various poetry collections and plays.

Books for children:
Winter King and Summer Queen
Princess Polly to the Rescue
Princess Polly and The Magic Megaplot
The Curse of the Macabres
Creepo Macabre and the Beast of Lock Horar

Printed in Great Britain
by Amazon